Penny Praise Ministries
Presents

Hoppin' John Celebrates Easter

Written by Penny Praise
Illustrated by Lauren Hodges

Scripture taken from the New King James Version. Copyright 1979, 1980, 1982 by Thomas Nelson, inc. Used by permission. All rights reserved.

WestBow Press books may be ordered through booksellers or by contacting:

WestBow Press
A Division of Thomas Nelson & Zondervan
1663 Liberty Drive
Bloomington, IN 47403
www.westbowpress.com
844-714-3454

ISBN: 978-1-4908-2287-7 (sc)
ISBN: 978-1-4908-2288-4 (e)

Library of Congress Control Number: 2014900727

Printed in the United States of America.

WestBow Press rev. date: 05/24/2023

WESTBOW
PRESS®
A DIVISION OF THOMAS NELSON
& ZONDERVAN

Acknowledgements

I am so deeply grateful for everyone who helped to make this book happen! First of all, I want to thank my husband, Miles, and our children, Amanda, Justen, and Scotty, and my sister, Misty Robertson, for all your support. Thanks also to Mike and Victoria Kelley, Meaghan Patrick and Lauren Hodges, and Mike and Lisa Brown, for all your hard work and creativity. Thanks to Miss Patty Cake for your inspiration and friendship through the years. And special thanks to Janice Tennet, Sandra Butler and Lecia Appling whose leadership, faith, and support we have all been blessed by. And to my whole Grove Family…You are AWESOME!!!

Dear Parents and Grandparents,

Thank you for loving your child and sharing God's Word with them. As you see, many pages have references on them to help you and your child understand where exactly in the Bible this story is told. I'm sure that your child will have questions (I hope so!) about Jesus' story. My hope is that those references will help you answer those questions with your child and lead you to an even better Bible study together.

Here are some points to consider as you read together:

- God's Word is always the Authority. Hoppin' John may be a fictional character, but he is no dumb bunny! He is a role model in showing that no matter how smart he is or how much he is respected by others, he will always lean on God's understanding rather than his own.
- Little Sparrow is a reminder that God loves and watches over all of us, no matter how small. His reference can be found in Matthew 10:29-31. And no question is too little when it leads us to greater understanding of Jesus Christ as our Lord and Savior.
- Jesus' birth is not just a historical event. It is also the fulfillment of Scripture going back many, many years before He was ever born into the world. It follows the logical progression of God delivering on His promises to us. Can your child guess why Mary might be winking in the manger scene? Could it be that she knows something the world doesn't know quite yet? Consider the biblical meaning of the baby donkey and lamb together with your child.
- Notice Jesus' finger pointing to the cross in the window frame at the Last Supper. Everything He said and did points to His sacrifice on the cross. That is what He tried to explain to His disciples that night. His disciples could not see the cross that lay ahead. Can your child see it? But the cross is not the end of the story, it is the beginning! Easter is about life, not death.
- In the company of an angel, Mary discovers Jesus' empty tomb and runs to tell everyone about it. Jesus is alive! Teach your child to tell everyone about Jesus. It will help strengthen your child in their own understanding and spread the Good News to others just as the angel said in Matthew 28:7.
- Notice how the old rugged wooden cross becomes a cross of gold over Jesus' heart. Through His sacrifice, a symbol of torture and death becomes a symbol of eternal love and everlasting life. We focus on the transformed cross as a measure of God's love for us, His children. His love and sacrifice create spiritual gold. Jesus wears purple as a sign of His royal kingship. He is Lord of all.

The things we surround ourselves with at Easter such as eggs, bunnies, baby animals and flowers are like signposts pointing us in the direction of the Risen Christ. The colored eggs remind us of the bright colorful new life awaiting us as Christians. The bunnies are a testament to how fast that life can multiply into new friends in the community of faith. A lamb reminds us of Jesus Christ, the Lamb of God and worthy sacrifice. The whole point of celebrating Easter is the celebration of life and life more abundant! Jesus says so in John 10:10.

If your child would like to accept Jesus Christ as his or her Lord and Savior, we have included a short, simple salvation prayer you and your child may wish to recite together. It may also serve as a conversation starter with your child on the kind of new life Christ calls us to. What does it mean to be saved?

As we teach our children the true meaning of Easter, remember to have fun! Children often learn best when the lesson is taught with joy and playtime is learning time.

May God Bless you!

Ms. Penny Praise

Hoppin' John is all dressed up for Easter.
A very special springtime celebration!

2 Corinthians 3:18

Hoppin' John meets with his friends.

Little Sparrow asks, "Why is Easter so special, Hoppin' John?"

Hoppin' John says, "Let me tell you what God says about Easter, Little Sparrow."

Deuteronomy 6:5-7

Many years ago, God sent His only son, Jesus, to us. God knew we needed a Savior to give us all new life because of our sins.

Isaiah 53
Luke 2:1-20

When Jesus grew up, He healed the sick.

"I can hear!"
"I can see!"
"I can walk!"

Isaiah 35:5-6
Matthew 11:5
John 5:5-9
John 9

Jesus told His friends He would have to leave, but He would come back.

Luke 24:7
John 14:1-4
John 15:12-15

Many people did not believe God sent Jesus to save us and give us new life.

Jesus willingly died for us all.

Jesus said, "Forgive them, Father. They don't understand."

Matthew 27:35-66
Luke 23:14-25
Luke 23:34
John 10:14-18
John 19:11

Jesus' friends laid Him in a tomb. Three days later, He rose again in new life!

"Jesus is alive!"

Matthew 27:59-63
Matthew 28:1-8
Luke 24:1-10

Just as Jesus is no longer on the cross, our sins are gone also.

We are forgiven.

Matthew 26:28
Colossians 2:12-14
James 5:15

When we accept that Jesus died and rose again for all of us, then we will have a new life, too!

Mark 16:15-19
John 10:9-11
Acts 1:9
Romans 8:38-39

Because Jesus gave us new life, we continue to celebrate His gift to us.

Easter eggs, bunnies, and baby animals all remind us of God's creation of new life.

Romans 6:4
2 Corinthians 5:17
1 Peter 2:2

Always remember the new life you have when you believe in Jesus!

John 3:16

Dear God,

I believe that your Son, Jesus, died and rose again to save me from sin. Please forgive me for my sins. I accept Jesus as my Savior, and I accept the new life He offers me. Thank you, God, for loving me so much!

In the Holy Name of Jesus Christ I pray,
Amen

Welcome to God's Family!!!

"Whoever calls on the name of the Lord shall be saved." (Romans 10:13)

Printed in the United States
by Baker & Taylor Publisher Services